D0502319

Series consultant: Brian Williams
Author: Steve Parker
Educational consultant: Barbara Reseigh
Illustrators: Brighton Illustration Agency (pages 14–20, 22–25, 36–39, 56–59, 98–99)
Kuo Kang Chen (page 13)
Nick Hawken (cover and pages 26–27, 48–51, 54–55, 60–61, 74–75, 80–85, 88–91, 104–106)
Barbara Lofthouse (page 53)
Shirley Mallinson (pages 52, 76–79, 92–93)
Denis Ryan (pages 94–97)
Stephen Seymour (pages 12, 44–47, 62–65, 70–71, 114–119)
John Spires (pages 28–31, 66–69, 86–87)
Graham White (pages 32–35, 40–41, 102–103)
ZEFA (page 107)

Designer: The Pinpoint Design Company
Editor: Camilla Hallinan

First American edition, 1993

Copyright © 1992 by Grisewood & Dempsey Ltd./Larousse Jeunesse.
All rights reserved under International and Pan-American Copyright
Conventions. Published in the United States by Random House, Inc.,
New York. Originally published in Great Britain by Kingfisher Books, a
Grisewood & Dempsey Company, and Larousse Jeunesse in 1992.

YOUNG WORLD is a trademark of Random House, Inc.

Library of Congress Cataloging in Publication Data
Parker, Steve.
    How things are made / by Steve Parker.
    —1st American ed.
        p.   cm.—(Young world; 2)
Includes index.
    Summary: Examines the natural and mechanical
processes that produce everyday objects, from the
dyeing of denim for jeans to the welding of steel for a
skyscraper.
    1. Manufactures—Juvenile literature.
[1. Manufactures.] I. Title. II. Series: Young world
(New York, N.Y.)
TS146.P36   1993
670—dc20   92–21676
                ISBN 0–679–83695–0
                ISBN 0–679–93695–5 (lib.bdg.)

Manufactured in Spain
1 2 3 4 5 6 7 8 9 10

YOUNG WORLD

How Things
Are Made

Random House **New York**

About YOUNG WORLD

For every young child, the world is full of new discoveries, new knowledge. It is important to have information books that enable even the youngest to enjoy making these discoveries and gathering this knowledge for themselves.

YOUNG WORLD introduces a wide range of the topics that absorb children. The books in this series are all carefully prepared by specialist authors with the help of experienced educational advisers and teachers so that information is presented simply and memorably. Each book is complete in itself, yet builds into a multi-volume set – a real encyclopedia for the vital first years at school.

Because YOUNG WORLD books are small and easy to handle, children can dip into them on their own or read them with the help of a parent or teacher. On each eye-catching page, a great deal of thought has been put into matching the clear, readable text with beautiful illustrations. These books are designed to encourage children to find facts for themselves, opening the door to a world where learning is fun.

Brian Williams, series consultant

About this book

Long ago, most people made their own clothes, tools, furniture, and dwellings. They collected food from the wild or grew their own crops and kept a few animals. They cooked and stored food too.

Today it is very different. We buy most of the things we need in stores and supermarkets. Often we do not know how something is made, or what it is made from, or who made it. This book shows us, by going out into the fields and factories and workshops. It explains how even a simple item such as a pencil involves the work of many people and machines. Next time you use a pencil, or eat a slice of bread, or put on a pair of jeans, you will know where it came from, and how it was made.

Steve Parker, author

CONTENTS

FOOD

AT HOME

OUT AND ABOUT

From start

to finish

How things are made

Animals and plants are living things. They are part of nature. But many things are not made naturally. People make them.

People built this tall skyscraper. People made this little package of peanuts. Who made them? What are they made of? How were they made?

This book tells you about all sorts of things and how they are made: clothes, food, things you use at home, things you see outside.

Different things are made in different ways.

Some things are made in factories,
by people working with robots and other
machines. Other things are made by
one person at home, using small tools.
But making anything requires:

careful planning,   the right materials,

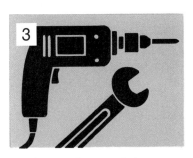

tools and machines   tests to make sure
to help,   things are made well.

🚲 Who designs a bike?

Many people take part in making a new bicycle.

The bicycle company wants to make a bike that will sell well. So market researchers ask children what kinds of bikes they like best.

Engineering designers draw the new bike, to show how it will work. Graphic designers choose popular colors and patterns for it.

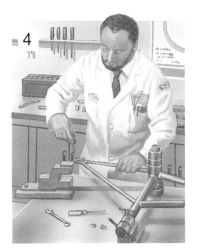

If the company likes the designers' plans for the new bike, models are built by hand.

These models are called prototypes. They show what the bike will look like.

The prototypes are tested to make sure the bike is safe and works well. Then the factory can make thousands of bikes like it.

🚲 What is a bike made of?

A bicycle has hundreds of parts, made of all sorts of materials.

The **seat** is made of plastic, with foam padding for comfort and a vinyl cover.

brake caliper
aluminum

tire
rubber

chain
steel

valve cap
plastic

valve
steel and brass

The parts come from factories in several countries around the world.

frame
a metal called
cromoly – a
type of steel

handlebar grip
rubber

brake lever
steel

brake cable
steel covered in nylon

fork
cromoly

spoke
steel

rim
aluminum

hub
aluminum

🚲 How is a bike made?

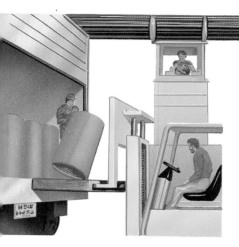

All the parts for the bicycles arrive at the factory.

Machines cut the long tubes of steel and bend them to make pieces for the frame.

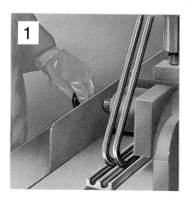

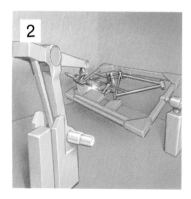

Next, the pieces are put together in the welding shop. A robot melts small patches of metal where the pieces are joined together. When the metal cools, it hardens and holds the frame together.

18

In the paint shop, the frame is sprayed with paint. In another part of the factory, spoking machines put spokes into the wheel hubs before the rims and tires go on.

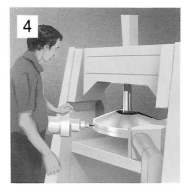

The frame is put on a moving assembly line. Fitters fix the forks and wheels onto the frame. Other fitters add the handlebars and all the other parts as the bike moves along.

🚲 Does this bike work?

A bike has to be safe, comfortable, and easy to ride. And it has to last. So first the prototypes are tested. Then all bikes are tested before they leave the factory and go on sale.

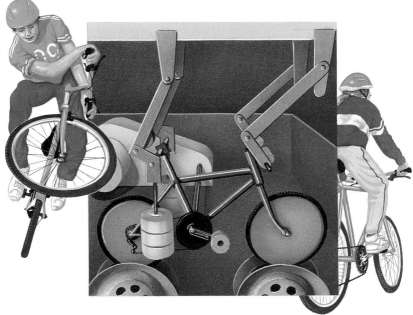

This prototype is being tested on rollers like bumpy cobblestones. A machine drives it at 25 miles per hour (that is how fast a car travels through a town), for 250 hours (that is about 10 days).

Clothes

The fashion designer

Some jeans are baggy, others are tight.
And blue is not the only color for jeans.
Designers decide on the style. They make
drawings of how the new jeans will look.

Designers' patterns show the shape of each
piece of material needed to make a pair of
jeans. Most jeans are made from a strong
type of cotton cloth called denim.

Cotton is made from the fluffy coverings of the seeds of cotton plants, called bolls.

Farmers collect the fluffy bolls with cotton harvesters.

cotton bolls

23

A pair of jeans

The cotton is cleaned and pressed into
bales. The bales are taken to a cotton mill.
There, spinning machines twist the cotton
into long threads and wind it onto reels.

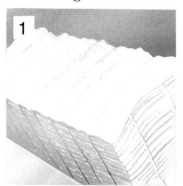

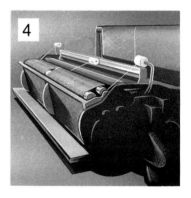

The cotton thread is soaked·in huge vats of
dye, to give it a blue color called indigo.
Then looms weave the thread into cloth.

At the jeans factory, cutters cut several layers of denim at once, with a long, sharp blade. A paper pattern on top shows the shape of each piece for a pair of jeans.

Then machinists sew the pieces together.

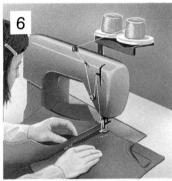

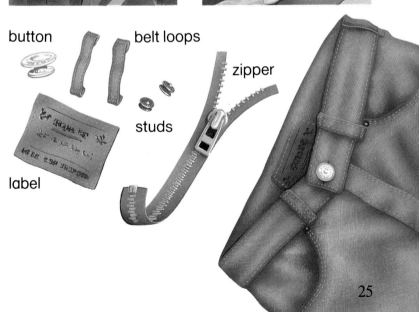

button

belt loops

zipper

studs

label

♠ A woolen sweater

Woolen clothes are made from the hair of animals such as sheep. The sheep's wool is called its fleece.

The shearer cuts the wool from the sheep with sharp clippers.

Shearing is like a haircut and does not hurt. The sheep soon grows a new fleece.

26

The wool is cleaned and spun into long threads called yarn. Then the wool is colored with dye.

People buy balls of yarn for knitting clothes.

This person is follow-ing a pattern for a sweater. It shows her how much yarn she needs and which kind of knitting needles and stitches to use.

27

 # Silk

silkworm

Silk is another material that comes from an animal. The silkworm is a caterpillar that spins a cocoon of silk around itself. It turns into a moth and hatches out from the cocoon.

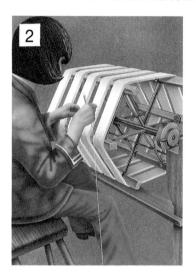

Farmers sell the cocoons to the silk factory.

At the factory, the cocoons are unraveled, and their silk is wound into thread on reeling frames. The thread is soaked in dye and woven into cloth on a loom.

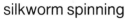
silkworm spinning

cocoon

adult moth

Silk is a beautiful material. It is used all over the world to make clothes for special occasions.

Japanese kimono, for festivals

Indian sari, for dancing

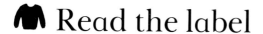 # Read the label

A label can tell you a lot about how something is made. Look at this label for a pair of jeans.

name of the manufacturer – the company that made the jeans

what they are made of

Blue Moon JEANS CO.

100% COTTON

60° WASH SEPARATELY

W 22in L 20in

MADE IN UNITED STATES

how they should be cleaned

what size they are

where they were made

Labels appear in different places on different things.

How many labels can you find here?

🖤 Made of plastic

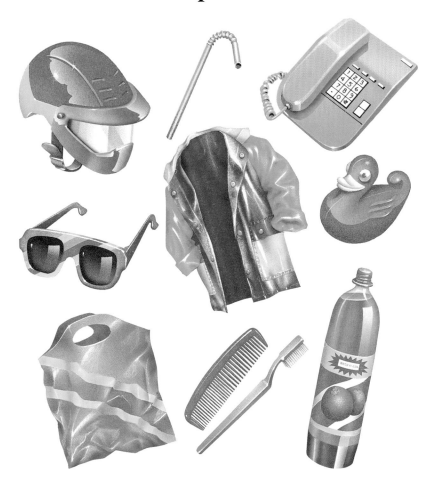

Thousands of things are made of plastic,
perhaps even some of your clothes.

rig

Plastic is made from oil.
Oil is found underground.
Giant rigs drill deep holes in
the ground. The oil flows up
the pipes inside the hole. It is
called crude oil. It goes by
pipeline or by tanker to the
oil refinery.

crude oil refinery

The refinery heats the crude oil
to separate the chemicals in it.
These chemicals make useful
things such as gasoline and
plastics.

There are many kinds of plastic
– hard plastics and soft,
bendable plastics. A soft plastic
called PVC is made from one of
the chemicals in crude oil and
from salt.

salt

33

A plastic raincoat

Tankers take dry PVC powder from the refinery to a chemical plant.

chemical to make the mixture soft

pigment, to add color

PVC powder

chemical to make the mixture last

PVC pellets

At the chemical plant, the PVC powder is mixed with other chemicals to make PVC pellets. The pellets are sold to factories that make things from PVC. Some raincoats are made from PVC.

First, the pellets are melted into a hot liquid.

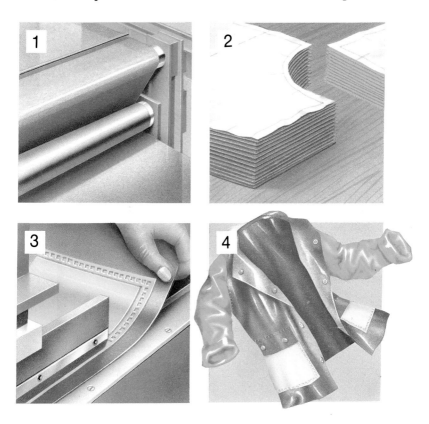

Rollers press the liquid into a thin sheet. The sheet hardens as it cools. Then it is cut into pieces. Instead of being sewn together, the pieces are pressed by a hot weight so they melt slightly and stick together.

 Shoes

We wear shoes every day: shoes with laces and shoes with buckles; shoes made of leather and shoes made of plastic; ballet shoes and sports shoes.

Look at how many pieces there are in just one sneaker. The pieces all have names.

The top of the shoe is called the upper.

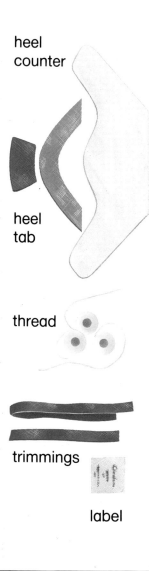

heel
counter

heel
tab

thread

trimmings

label

36

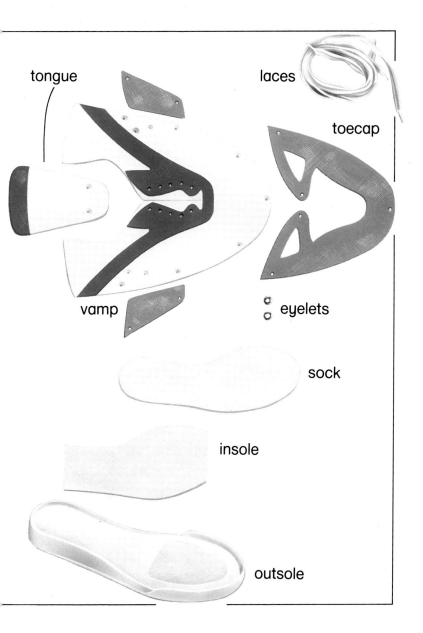

tongue

laces

toecap

vamp

eyelets

sock

insole

outsole

37

The shoemakers

A cutter cuts out the pieces for the upper.
A machinist sews them together. Holes and
eyelets for the shoelaces are punched. Then
another machinist attaches the insole.

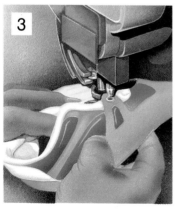

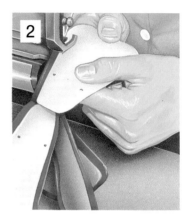

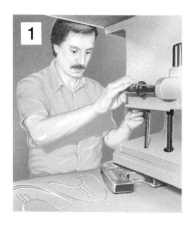

The upper is put on a model of a foot called a last. The last is lowered into a mold which is filled with hot liquid plastic. As the plastic cools, it becomes a hard sole for the shoe. Then a lining called the sock is glued in. Inspectors check that shoes are well made.

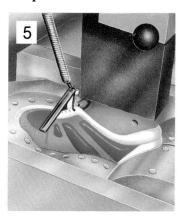

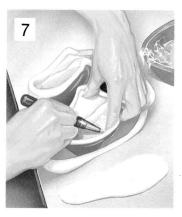

quality control inspector

 # A watch

This small watch contains 30 parts made in 5 different countries.

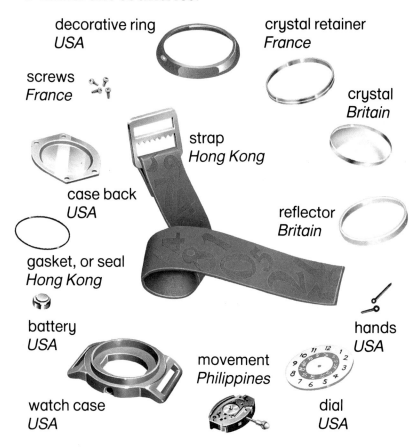

decorative ring
USA

crystal retainer
France

screws
France

crystal
Britain

strap
Hong Kong

case back
USA

reflector
Britain

gasket, or seal
Hong Kong

battery
USA

hands
USA

movement
Philippines

watch case
USA

dial
USA

The movement is a set of gears and wheels that turn the hands. The battery keeps it working.

A designer draws the watch on a computer.
Machines make the parts such as the dial.
Then the assembler puts them together.
A magnifying lens helps him to see even
the tiniest parts.

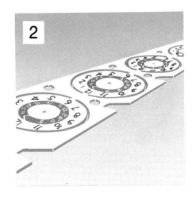

The watch is tested. It is even put in water,
to make sure that it keeps working.

Amazing facts

The first denim jeans were made for cowboys, farmers, and other workers in the U.S. about 100 years ago.

A good shearer can cut the fleeces of between 150 and 200 sheep in one day.

Wool comes not just from sheep but from goats, camels, yaks, llamas, and rabbits.

One silkworm can make nearly 5,000 feet of silk thread in its cocoon.

Watch straps were invented about 100 years ago. Before that, people carried watches in their pockets.

Food

On the farm

Many of the foods we eat are grown on farms and then prepared in factories. This is the story of peanuts. In the spring, farmers plow the fields and plant peanut seeds.

The peanuts ripen just below the surface, inside their shells. A digger-shaker pulls the plants out of the ground.

A spreader adds fertilizers, to help the peanut plants to grow. Like the plow and the seed drill, the spreader is pulled by a tractor. The plants need a lot of water while they grow. So, during the hot summer, an irrigator sprinkles water over the field.

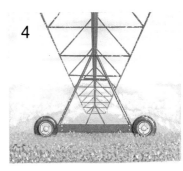

The combine pulls the peanuts off the plants and empties them into a big trailer. The farmer sells the peanuts to a factory.

Roasted peanuts

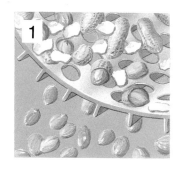

At the factory, the peanuts are shaken on grates so that their shells break apart and the nuts fall out.

Factory workers and electronic sorting machines check the peanuts. They take out any bad nuts and bits of shell and grit.

More machines weigh the peanuts into large sacks.

Some nuts are sold to other factories that make peanut butter and roasted peanuts.

Before peanuts are roasted, they are sometimes blanched. Blanching heats the peanuts to make their red skins split open. Metal rollers shake the peanuts so the skins fall off.

Peanuts are roasted in hot oil for about five minutes, at 300 degrees Fahrenheit.

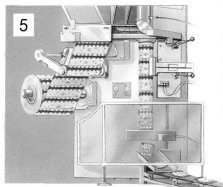

The roasted nuts are weighed and wrapped by a bagging machine.

ready for the stores

Growing wheat

Most of the bread we eat is made from wheat. Farmers grow wheat in huge fields.

When the wheat is ripe, a combine harvester collects the seeds, called grain.

grain

The wheat grain is stored in huge silos until it is sold to a flour mill.

At the mill, the grain is crushed and ground into fine flour.

Tankers take the flour from the mill to the bakery, to be made into bread.

flour

49

At the bakery

Bread is usually made from four main ingredients: flour, water, salt, and yeast.

The ingredients are poured into a high-speed mixer.

The mixer stirs the ingredients into a soft dough. Next, a divider cuts the dough into lumps called loaves. The loaves are put on trays and taken to a warm place called a prover, to make the dough rise or swell up. Then the dough is cooked in a huge hot oven and becomes bread.

After it is cooked, the bread is lifted off the trays by suction pads. Some bread is sliced and wrapped by machine. Then trucks take the bread to the stores.

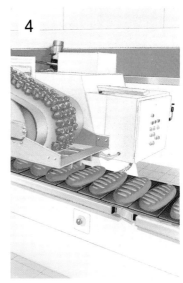

All kinds of bread

Bread can be made from different types of flour and baked in different ways. So there are many kinds of bread around the world.

These bakers are making bread by hand and cooking it in a small oven. The bread is flat because the dough has no yeast.

Have you ever eaten any of these breads?

hamburger bun

roti

matzos

sliced bread

bagel

croissant

pumpernickel

pita

baguette

pizza

People make flour from these plants.

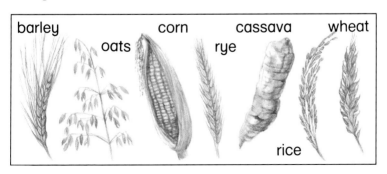

barley

oats

corn

rye

cassava

wheat

rice

Breakfast cereal

Cornflakes are made from sweet corn. When the corn has ripened in the sun, farmers harvest their crop.

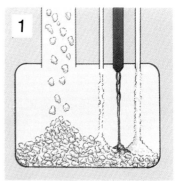

2

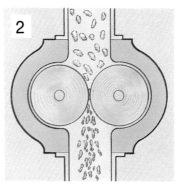

1

Grains of corn are stripped from the plants and taken to a cereal factory. At the factory, sugar, salt, and malt flavoring are added to the corn to give it extra taste. Next, the mixture is cooked. Then heavy rollers press the corn into flakes.

The flakes are toasted in giant ovens to make them crispy.

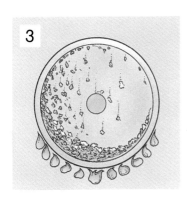

Filling machines weigh the cornflakes into bags. The bags are sealed to keep the cornflakes fresh.

Conveyor belts take the bags to be packed in boxes. The boxes are put in big cardboard cartons, to protect them on their way to the stores.

Milking time

Cows make milk to feed their calves. Farmers keep herds of cows to produce milk for people as well.

The cows come into the milking parlor twice a day.

Milking takes about ten minutes.
The herdsman fits cups connected to pipes
over the cows' teats. When the cups gently
squeeze the teats, a milking machine sucks
the milk from each cow's udder.

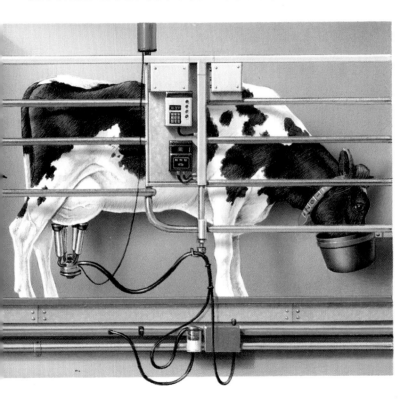

The milk flows through the pipes to a cold
tank, to keep it fresh while it is on the farm.

At the dairy

A milk tanker collects the milk from the
farm each day and delivers it to a dairy.

At the dairy, technicians test samples of the
milk. It must be fresh enough to sell.

If it passes the tests, the milk is quickly
heated and cooled inside huge tanks. This
is called pasteurization. It kills any germs
in the milk and makes it safe to drink.

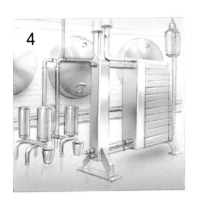

1-quart
carton

half-gallon container

1-pint carton   1-pint bottle

Filling machines squirt the milk into plastic
containers, cardboard cartons, and glass bottles.

Made of milk

Milk from the dairy is used to make all of these foods. That is why they are called dairy products.

chocolate

ice cream

butter

yogurt

cheese

cream

All over the world, farmers keep animals that produce milk for people to use.

reindeer

goat

llama

camel

yak

sheep

Tea

Tea plants are grown in warm, wet lands such as Asia and East Africa.

Tea pickers pull off the top leaves. The leaves are shredded and left in the air to soften until they change color from green to brown. Then the leaves are dried and packed into chests.

4

Ships carry chests of tea to tea factories around the world. At the factory, a tea taster makes cups of tea from different batches of leaves. He decides on the best mixture, or blend, of leaves.

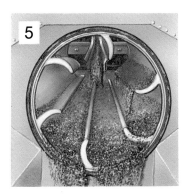

5

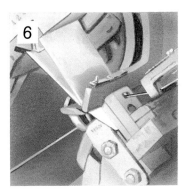

6

A rotating drum mixes large amounts of the blend. Then a bagging machine measures the leaves into pockets of tissue paper and seals the edges, to make tea bags. Some tea is packed in cans and boxes instead.

a cup of tea

🐂 Fizzy drinks

Oranges and other fruit give many fizzy drinks a delicious taste. Pickers pull the fruit from the trees.

Juice is squeezed from the fruit and packed in drums.

Ships take the juice to other countries.

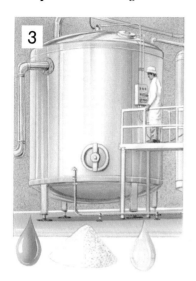

At the factory, sugar, water, and other ingredients are added to the juice. In a high-pressure tank, a gas called carbon dioxide is forced into the mixture, to give it sparkling bubbles.

A can-filling machine squirts the drink into 8,000 cans each minute. A machine called a seamer puts the lids on.

🐄 A soda can

Cans are made of metal, often a metal called steel. Steel comes from iron ore under the ground. Miners dig up the ore.

At the steel mill, huge furnaces heat the iron ore to turn it into liquid iron and then liquid steel. As the liquid cools and hardens, rolling mills flatten it into sheets of steel. Factories buy the steel to make cans.

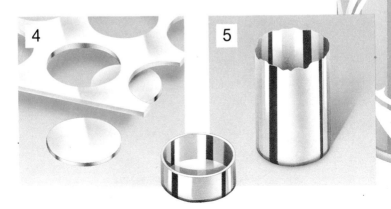

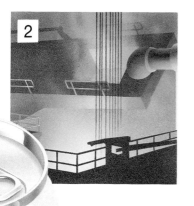

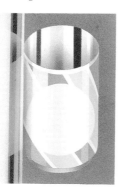

At the factory, a press pushes small disks out of the steel sheet. An ironing machine stretches each disk into a can shape. Printing rollers add color. Another machine shapes the top of the can where the lid will fit.

Wrapping it up

Manufacturers – the people who make things – package most food before it goes to the stores. They put it in boxes and cartons, bags and cans, jars and bottles. Some packaging is made of plastic, some of glass, and some of paper and cardboard.

What is packaging for?
• Packaging helps to protect food and keep it fresh.
• Packaging makes food easy to store in the shops and easy to take home.
• Packaging helps customers see what they are buying. It gives them information about what is inside.
• Food is packaged in different sizes, so customers can buy the amount they need.

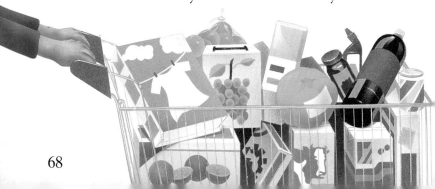

Designers plan how to package food in the best way.

Fish sticks would not fit in a bottle or a jar or a can. They might get squashed in a plastic bag.

A cardboard box is best. It is the right shape. It will protect the fish sticks. And it is not too heavy.

A plain box would look boring, and it would not show what is inside. It needs a design.

Most of the things we buy have packaging for the same reasons.

🐄 Fish sticks

Trawler boats pull huge nets through the ocean to catch fish. Then the nets are hauled on board. Trawlermen pack the fish in boxes of ice, to keep them fresh.

Fish stick manufacturers buy the fish.

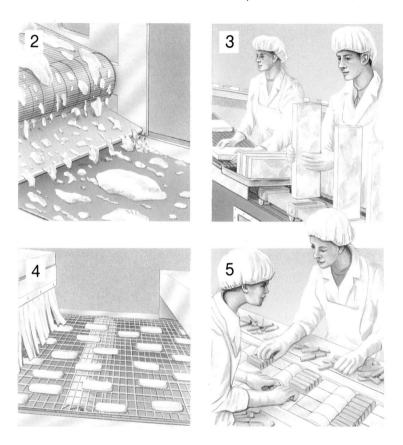

A filleting machine cuts the flesh off the bones. The fish is frozen in large blocks. These are sliced up, coated with bread-crumbs, and cooked in hot oil. Then the fish sticks are packed in cardboard boxes.

Amazing facts

Peanuts are not just good to eat. They are also used to make shaving cream, washing powder, soap, and ink!

One large bakery can make 10,000 loaves of bread each hour.

A cow can give as much as 2 gallons of milk in one milking.

A tea picker collects about 65 pounds of leaves in one day. That is enough for about 20 boxes of tea bags.

In 1809, a Frenchman named Nicolas Appert was the first person to put food in cans. He won a competition to invent a way of keeping food fresh for soldiers fighting in the Napoleonic Wars.

More sardines and herrings are caught to eat than any other fish. Most fish sticks are made from fish called cod.

At home

Timber from the forest

Timber, or wood, comes from trees in the forest. Lumberjacks cut down the trees with chainsaws. Young trees are planted to replace the trees that have been cut down.

Logging trucks take the wood to a sawmill.

The bark is cut away from the trunks, and then the wood is sawed into planks.
The wood is sold, to be made into chairs, pencils, paper, and many other things.

The carpenter

Some carpenters are craftsmen and craftswomen who make chairs and other furniture out of beautiful pieces of wood.

First, the carpenter chooses which kind of wood he wants to use for a chair. Then he draws each part of the chair onto the wood.

For the chair legs, the carpenter uses a lathe to turn the wood while he cuts it to the right shape with a sharp metal gouge. Most woodworking tools are made of metal. They must be kept sharp.

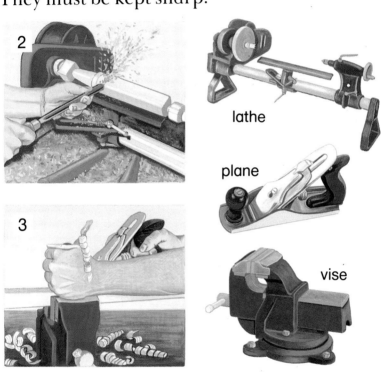

lathe

plane

vise

The carpenter puts the wood in a vise to hold it steady. He shaves off bits of wood with a plane, to smooth some of the pieces.

☕ A chair takes shape

This is the back support. A sharp drawknife cuts the wood to make the curved shape.

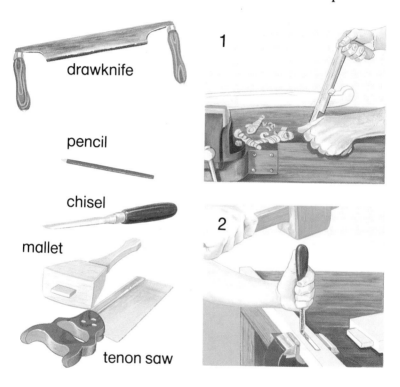

drawknife

pencil

chisel

mallet

tenon saw

1

2

The carpenter saws the ends of some pieces to make joints. On other pieces he carves a matching hole for each joint to fit into. Without joints, the chair would fall apart.

The carpenter puts some glue into the joints
and fits the pieces together. A clamp holds
the chair until the glue has dried.

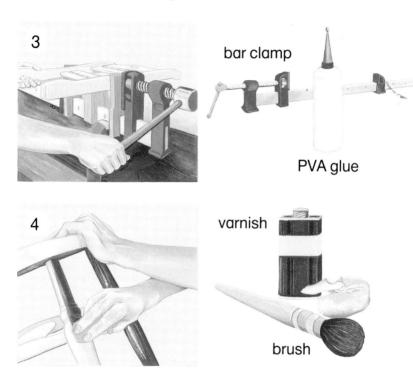

3

bar clamp

PVA glue

4

varnish

brush

Then the carpenter wipes varnish onto the
chair and polishes it when the varnish is
dry. Varnish helps to protect the wood and
gives it a nice shine.

☕ Parts for pencils

Pencils are made of wood, clay, and graphite.

clay

graphite

cedar
wood

Clay lies just under the ground. Big excavators dig it out, and blasting machines crush it into fine powder with jets of water.

Graphite is a soft
black rock, deep
under the ground.

Miners remove the
graphite with drills.
The wood comes from
cedar trees.

☕ Making pencils

Graphite and clay are mixed into a paste.
For colored pencils, dye is added to the
paste. Next, the paste is squeezed into long
thin pieces called leads. Then the leads are
baked until they are hard.

Saws cut the cedar wood into pieces called slats. Glue sticks a lead into each groove in one slat. Another slat is glued on top.

Then the slats are sawed into separate pencils. A huge rotating frame dips the pencils in paint to coat the wood.

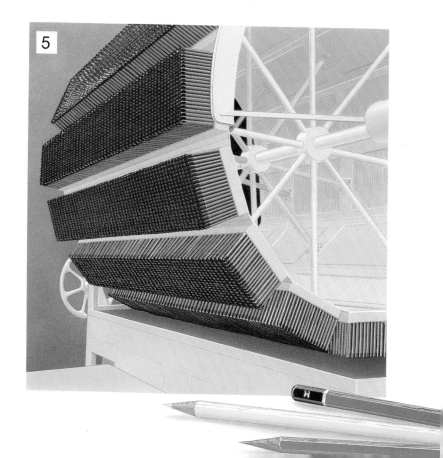

🥤 At the paper mill

The main woods used to make paper are fir, spruce, and pine. This is how some paper is made. First, the bark is taken off the logs. Then chipping machines cut up the logs.

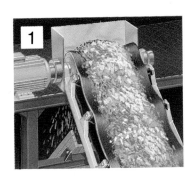

The wood chips are cooked with chemicals in a mixing machine called a digester. This turns the chips into a pasty pulp.

Then the pulp is cleaned and rinsed with water. The pulp is spread on a moving wire screen, and most of the water drips away. Heavy rollers press the pulp into a very thin sheet and squeeze out more water. Hot rollers dry the paper.

Finally, the paper is wound onto a roll called a reel. It is sold to make books, newspapers, and many other things.

Old for new

A lot of the materials that manufacturers use are recycled materials. Recycling means using old things again instead of throwing them away.

For example, steel is recycled. Making things with old steel helps the manufacturer save money, because less new steel is used. Old ships, cars, even cans at the garbage dump can be recycled.

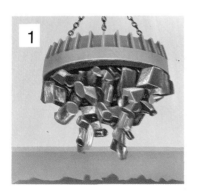

After the garbage has been burned, a big magnet picks out any steel cans. The cans are crushed into bales and sent to the steel mill. Old steel is called scrap.

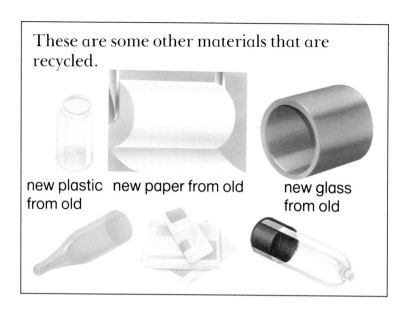

These are some other materials that are recycled.

new plastic from old   new paper from old   new glass from old

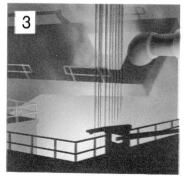

At the steel mill, the bales of scrap are melted down in a furnace to make new steel. A quarter of the steel in every soda can comes from recycled steel.

☕ At the glassworks

The main ingredients in glass are a type of
sand called silica, bits of scrap glass called
cullet, soda ash, and limestone. They are
mixed together and heated in a furnace
until they melt and turn into molten glass.

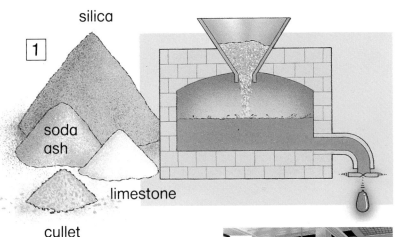

silica

1

soda
ash

limestone

cullet

2

Rollers press the hot
liquid glass into a flat
sheet. The glass
hardens as it cools.
It is used to make
windowpanes.

Glass jars and bottles are made in a different way.

As the molten glass flows from the furnace, it is cut into blobs called gobs. Each gob drops into a mold.

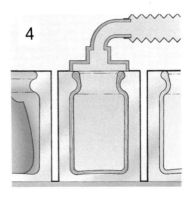

A blast of air presses the glass against the sides of this mold, in the shape of a jar.

The mold opens. Tongs pick up the jar and put it into a big oven called a lehr. The lehr heats the glass again, to make it stronger.

🍵 The glass blower

Some glass is made by hand. This is a skilled job.

The gatherer picks up a gob of molten glass on a long tube.

The blower blows down the tube to fill the gob with air and make it swell up like a balloon.

90

The blower keeps turning the tube so the glass doesn't drip off. He squeezes the end of the gob with tongs, to make a long stem. The foot setter adds another gob to the stem and flattens it into a base called a foot.

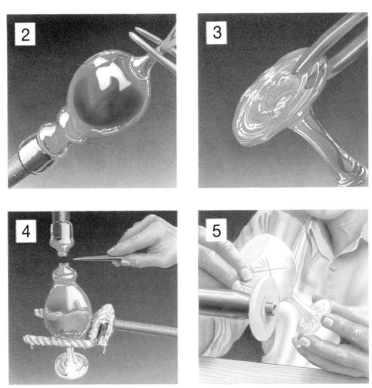

The cutter takes the glass and smooths it with a grinder. He cuts the glass with a sharp, whirring wheel to make a pattern.

🍵 Pottery

The potter puts a lump of wet clay on a flat
wheel. As the wheel turns, the potter shapes
the clay with her hands. This is called
throwing. The potter here is throwing
a mug. She adds a handle.

The mug goes into an oven called a kiln.

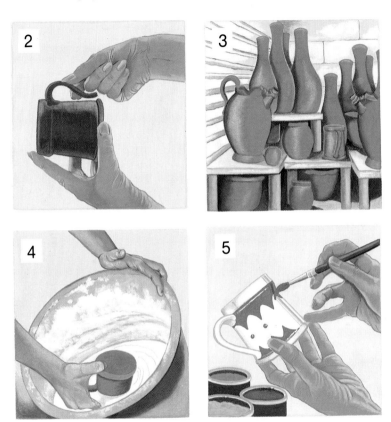

The kiln makes the clay hard by firing, or baking, it. Then the potter coats the mug with a shiny glaze, to protect it and make it water-proof. She fires the mug again, decorates it with paint, and fires it one more time.

🎥 The film crew

These people are making a program about animals. The producer plans the story and pictures and the filming expedition. Researchers find out about the animals and the best places, or locations, for filming them.

On location, the producer and his assistant make sure the film crew is ready. The  narrator reads a script that tells the story. The sound engineer tapes the sounds. The camera operator takes the pictures. Wild animals are shy, so they are hard to film. The camera operator has worked alone for months to get good pictures.

In the television studio

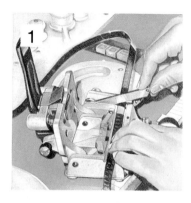

When the film crew returns from location, the film is developed with chemicals to reveal the pictures. A film editor cuts out strips of film that show the best scenes. She joins them together to make a good story.

A sound editor chooses the tape recordings that match the pictures.

An assistant runs the tapes while the editor views the pictures on a screen. He presses buttons on the control console in front of him to choose the right sounds. Matching sounds and pictures is called dubbing, or mixing.

4

5

The television program is broadcast from the studio. It travels as invisible signals to a transmitting station. Transmitters make the signals strong enough to reach television antennas. Now the penguins are on television!

97

🥄 Toothpaste

Toothpaste is made from this mixture:

• hydrated silica, to polish your teeth,

• sorbitol, made from plants, for binding the mixture into a paste,

• a foaming agent, to make the toothpaste frothy,

• mint, or other flavors, for a fresh taste and smell,

• water, to turn the mixture into a soft paste,

• and fluoride, to help prevent tooth decay.

FLUORIDE

The ingredients are mixed in a vat and poured into tubes. A red light shows when each tube is full. Then the tubes are closed and packed in cartons.

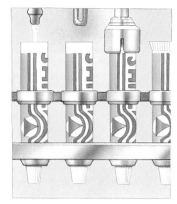

In striped toothpaste, colored paste is put in first. Then white paste fills the rest of the tube.

When you squeeze the tube, the white paste comes out through a nozzle in the center, and the colored paste comes through holes around the edge.

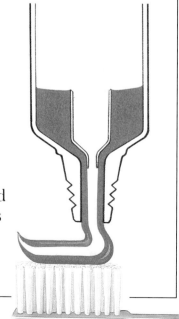

Amazing facts

) One pencil factory can make half a million pencils each day.

The first paper was made from reed plants in ancient Egypt over 5,000 years ago. The word "paper" comes from the name of the reeds, papyrus.

A big furnace contains over 440 tons of molten glass, which is the same weight as 10 tractor-trailer trucks.

) The first wheels ever made were potters' wheels. Wheels for carts and other kinds of transportation were invented later.

Out and

about

 # Postage stamps

When the postal service decides to bring out a new stamp, it chooses a theme – such as birds. Then artists design the stamp.

cyan
(blue)

magenta
(red)

yellow

10

black

4-color **10**

If the postal service likes a design, the artist paints artwork in color.

The artwork is photo-graphed onto film. A different film is made for each of the main colors. This is called reproduction.

Each film is copied onto a metal plate. The plates go to the printers.

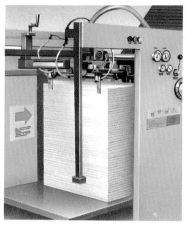
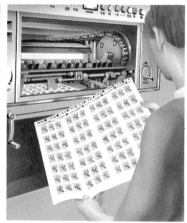

The printers load sheets of paper into a big machine called a printing press. The press copies each plate onto the paper, one color on top of another. A perforating machine pricks holes around each stamp. A guillotine slices the proofs into smaller sheets, ready for the post office.

At the mint

Making a new coin is like making a new stamp. First, a theme is chosen.
This coin is going to show the king of Spain.

An artist designs the new coin. Her designs show the pictures, numbers, and letters on both sides of the coin.

Look at how big the artist's drawing is. This is so she can fit a lot of detail into her design for the tiny coin. The designs are sent to the mint. The mint is where coins are made.

At the mint, drawing machines copy the designs to the right size, but back to front, on two blocks of steel. The blocks are called dies.

dies

Coins are made of mixtures of metals, called alloys. The mint buys bars of different metals. The bars are melted in a furnace and rolled into thin sheets.

Small disks called blanks are punched out of the sheets. Leftover metal from the sheets goes back to the furnace for recycling.

Striking the coin

The blanks are heated in another furnace, to make them soft. They are called blanks because they have no pattern yet.

A coining press squeezes each blank between the two metal dies. The blank is soft, so each die dents the blank with its pattern. This is called striking, or minting, the coins.

quality control inspector

106

All kinds of coins

Each country makes its own coins with its own designs. So there are many kinds of coins – coins made of different metals, in many shapes and sizes, and worth different amounts of money. Do you recognize any of these coins?

A new car

Car companies want to make new cars that are better and more popular than the cars already on sale. It costs a lot of money to design and make a new car. So companies need to know what kind of car will sell well.

Market researchers ask people what kind of car they want. Comfortable and safe? Sleek and speedy? Red, or another color?

Designers make sketches and engineers use computers to decide the size and shape of the new car.

Engineers build models by hand, to see if plans for the new car are good enough. First they make small models with clay or wood, then models the same size as a real car.

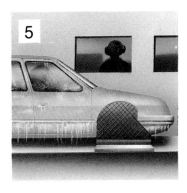

Next they build prototypes with the real materials, to test the car.

Prototypes with dummies at the wheel are crashed into walls, to see how safe the car is. Prototypes are also kept in ice-cold rooms and in very hot rooms, to make sure the car will work in bad weather.

On the assembly line

sheet steel

The main parts for the car body are made from sheet steel. A huge press shapes the steel into car doors and other parts.

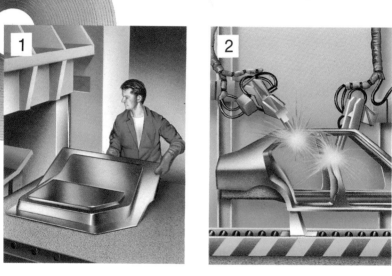

The parts are put together in the welding shop. Robots are programmed by computer to melt small patches of metal in each part. The patches stick together as the metal cools and hardens. This is called spot-welding.

The moving assembly line takes the car from the welding shop to the paint shop.

First the car is dipped in a pool of anti-rust paint. Then robots spray the car with color. A wax coating is added, to protect the paint from scratches and to make the car shiny.

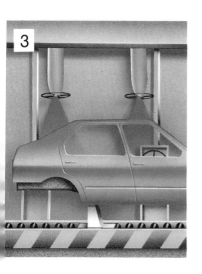 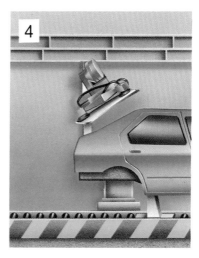

When the car comes out of the paint shop, robots with big suction pads fit the glass windshields. Robots move like human arms and hands. They do work that is too heavy, dangerous, or boring for people to do.

The fitters

As the car moves along the assembly line, assembly workers fit the other parts.

The car is lowered onto the engine and the chassis. The car is also tilted sideways.

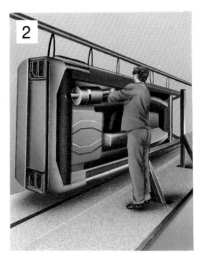

This makes it easier for fitters to connect the fuel tank and the exhaust pipe. More fitters add dozens of other parts. At the end of the assembly line, drivers test the finished car, to make sure it is ready to go on sale.

How many of these parts can you name?

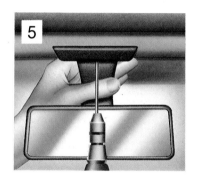

 A skyscraper

Architects and planners make the drawings and designs for a new skyscraper.

All the plans are checked: by people from the local area, to make sure the new skyscraper will fit in with its surroundings; by the people who are paying for the new skyscraper; and by the engineers and the construction company who will build it.

Model makers build a miniature version, to show what the sky-scraper will look like.

Surveyors measure the site. Engineers drill
into the soil and rock underneath, to check
its strength.

Demolition cranes knock
down old buildings, and
bulldozers clear away
the rubble.

🚗 On site

When the site has been
cleared, building can
begin. First, drills make
giant holes deep in
the ground.

Wet concrete and long pieces of steel are put in the holes. These are foundations to support the skyscraper above. Next, the steel frame goes up, piece by piece.

Walls and windows are fastened to the frame. Then the insides are finished.

We built it!

architect   engineer   surveyor

construction workers

It takes years to build a skyscraper, and the skills of hundreds of men and women.

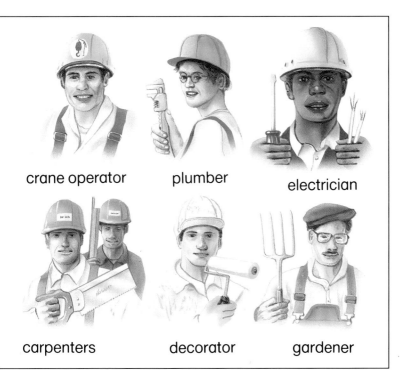

crane operator

plumber

electrician

carpenters

decorator

gardener

Yet building a tall skyscraper involves the same steps as making a small bike: careful planning; the right materials, tools, and machines; and tests to make sure it is made well and safe.

Amazing facts

Printing presses can print more than two million stamps every hour.

Silver coins are not made from silver, but from an alloy, or mixture, of the metals copper and nickel.

A family car contains more than 20,000 parts.

The tallest skyscraper in the world is the Sears Tower in Chicago, Illinois. It has 110 floors and is 1,454 feet high.

The editor would like to thank the many companies and individuals who assisted in the preparation of this book, including the following:
Alcoa, Sue Alexander, Alfa-Laval Agri Ltd, Anglia Television Ltd, APV Baker Ltd, Atlantic Mills Ltd, BBC Natural History Unit, Berol Ltd, Boyd Line Ltd, Bovis Construction Ltd, British Paper and Board Industry Federation, The British Soft Drinks Association Ltd, British Steel plc, Britvic Soft Drinks Ltd, Camelot, CMB Packaging Technology plc, CVJ Clark Ltd, Coca-Cola and Schweppes Beverages Ltd, Elida Gibbs Ltd, European Vinyls Corporation (UK) Ltd, Fabrica Nacional de Moneda y Timbre, The Fulham Pottery, GT Bicycles, Harrison & Sons Limited, Hoechst (UK) Ltd, Japan National Tourist Organization, Kellogg Company of Great Britain Ltd, KHS Klockner Holstein Seitz Ltd, Levi Strauss (UK) Ltd, Nacanco, National Dairy Council, National Peanut Council of America, The Parnham Trust, The Public Relations Business, Raleigh Industries Ltd, Rank Hovis McDougall, Renault Communications, Rockware Glass Ltd, The Rolex Watch Company Limited, Royal Mail Stamps, Saab Automobile AB, Salma International Ltd, Sea Fish Industry Authority, Shilland & Co, Silk Education Service, Smith & Nephew Textiles Ltd, Staedtler (UK) Ltd, Timex Corporation, Walsall Security Printers, Josiah Wedgwood and Sons Ltd, Elaine Willis, Wimpey, Woodworking*today* and Wrangler Ltd.

INDEX